WHEN WERE THE FIRST SLAVES SET FREE DURING THE CIVIL WAR?

And Other Questions about the Emancipation Proclamation

Shannon Knudsen

LERNER PUBLICATIONS COMPANY · MINNEAPOLIS

A Word about Language

English word usage, spelling, grammar, and punctuation have changed over the centuries. We have preserved original spellings and word usage in the quotations included in this book.

Lerner Publications Company
A division of Lerner Publishing Group, Inc.
241 First Avenue North
Minneapolis, MN 55401 U.S.A.

Website address: www.lernerbooks.com

Library of Congress Cataloging-in-Publication Data

Knudsen, Shannon, 1971–
    When were the first slaves set free during the Civil War? : and other questions
about the Emancipation Proclamation / by Shannon Knudsen.
        p. cm. — (Six questions of American history)
    Includes bibliographical references and index.
    ISBN 978–1–58013–670–9 (lib. bdg. : alk. paper)
    1. United States. President (1861–1865 : Lincoln). Emancipation Proclamation—
Juvenile literature. 2. Lincoln, Abraham, 1809–1865—Juvenile literature.
3. Slaves—Emancipation—United States—Juvenile literature. 4. United States—
Politics and government—1861–1865—Juvenile literature. I. Title.
E453.K68 2011
973.7'14—dc22   2009030527

Manufactured in the United States of America
1 – DP – 7/15/10

TABLE OF CONTENTS

.... 4

THE SIX QUESTIONS HELP YOU DISCOVER THE FACTS!

INTRODUCTION

The president's hand trembled as he held his gold pen. It was January 1, 1863, New Year's Day. Abraham Lincoln had just spent three hours shaking hands with visitors. His arm had gone numb. And he couldn't keep his hand steady. Lincoln didn't want to sign the document on his desk with a weak, shaky scrawl. People might think he had doubts. In fact, he knew he was doing the right thing. Finally, the president's pen touched the paper. He signed his name—and made history.

The document's name was a mouthful: the Emancipation Proclamation. The word *emancipation* means "setting someone free." A proclamation is an official announcement. The Emancipation Proclamation was an official announcement that freed slaves in parts of the United States. These slaves lived in the South. The southern states had left the United States in 1861.They had started a new country called the Confederate States of America. The northern states, called the Union, went to war against the Confederate States to make them return.

When Lincoln signed the Emancipation Proclamation, the North and the South had been fighting the Civil War for almost two years. How and why did slavery become such an important part of the U.S. way of life?

Facing page: President Abraham Lincoln (third from left) reads his Emancipation Proclamation to his advisers. This scene was painted by Francis Bicknell Carpenter in 1864.

FREE
STATE

TERRITORY

SLAVE
STATE

THE DIVIDED
NATION
1863

A copy of the
Emancipation Proclamation

WHO
WHAT
WHERE
WHY
WHEN
HOW
WHO
WHAT
WHERE
WHY
HOW
WHO
WHERE
WHY
WHEN
HOW

Slaves were crammed aboard ships sailing for the Americas. The slave trade lasted for hundreds of years.

ONE A NATION WITH SLAVES

people who come from certain long-ago family members

By the 1860s, Africans and their descendants had been slaves in North America for more than two hundred years. Starting in the 1600s, European and American traders brought thousands of Africans across the Atlantic Ocean. They were packed into ships like livestock. Those who survived the journey were sold.

animals kept and raised on a farm

Greed was one reason African people were enslaved. Slave traders could make a great deal of money by selling human beings. Slave owners got free labor. Another reason was racism. Most slave traders and owners were white. They claimed that their race was better than others. They thought they should rule over the Africans.

In the northern colonies, most white people lived in cities and towns or on small farms. Most slaves in these places worked as house servants or field hands.

settlements in a distant country

Their labor was important to their owners. But many white people also worked for pay as servants or hired hands in the North.

The southern colonies were different. By the 1800s, some slaves there worked in houses and on small farms. But most slaves worked on plantations. These huge farms produced many crops. Their owners needed many workers. The plantation owners bought slaves to get cheap labor.

These slaves work on a cotton plantation in the American South.

At slave auctions, like this one depicted by Friedrich Schulz in the 1800s, slaves were sold to whites. Families were frequently separated. Family members were sold off to different plantation owners.

LIFE AS A SLAVE

Slaves worked hard. Plantation slaves started work at first light. Their days didn't end until twelve to fourteen hours later. "I never knowed what it was to rest," a former slave named Sarah Gudger recalled. "I just work all de time from mornin' till late at night....Work in de field, chop wood, hoe corn, till sometimes I feels like my back surely break...." Children worked beside the adults. Slave owners often whipped those who didn't work fast enough.

Owners even used their slaves' children for labor. Sometimes owners beat their slaves to force them to work and obey. Owners could also sell their slaves at any time. Children could be sold away from their parents. Wives and husbands could be sold away from each other. Parents could be sold away from their children as well.

Many slaves took terrible risks to gain freedom. Some ran away to live with Native

Americans. Others escaped to places such as Canada. They believed they would be safe there. Some took up arms against their owners and fought for their lives. A few even tried to gain their freedom through the courts. For most slaves, these efforts did not succeed. And for many, they led to brutal punishments or even death.

During the Revolutionary War (1775–1783), American colonists went to war against Great Britain. White colonists wanted to win freedom from British rule. But few of them believed that Africans and African Americans should be freed from slavery. In fact, every British colony in North America permitted slavery at that time.

people who live in or help to start a colony

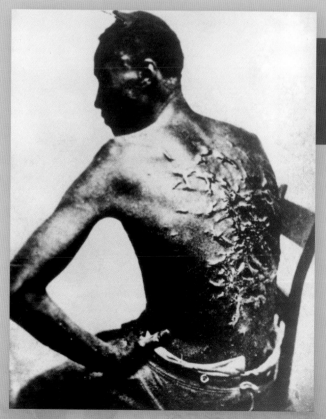

This slave was whipped as punishment for running away from his owner's plantation. He has scars on his back from the whipping he received.

Some white people did change their minds about slavery during the Revolutionary War. This happened mostly in the North. Slave labor wasn't as important there as it was in the South. People began to ask how the new nation could be built on freedom when so many of its people had no freedom at all. In 1777 Vermont banned slavery. One by one, other parts of the North followed.

outlawed; to have a rule against certain actions or things

In the South, slavery remained strong. Southern plantation owners had no way to plant and harvest crops without many workers. And the cheapest way to get workers was still to own people.

In 1787 men from every state met in the city of Philadelphia, Pennsylvania. These men were called delegates.

In this hand-colored engraving, George Washington leads the discussion during the 1787 Constitutional Convention.

They represented their states. The delegates talked about a new constitution, a plan for the government of the United States. The question of slavery turned out to be one of their biggest disagreements. Some delegates from the North wanted to outlaw slavery. But delegates from the South said that their states wouldn't be part of the United States unless slavery was allowed.

The northern delegates decided to compromise. Slavery was not directly mentioned in the U.S. Constitution. It remained legal in any state that allowed it. And hundreds of thousands of Africans and African Americans remained trapped in suffering. But some people did try to stop slavery.

to come to an agreement

NEXT QUESTION

WHO WERE THE PEOPLE WHO WERE TRYING TO STOP SLAVERY?

WHO
WHAT
WHERE
WHY
WHEN
HOW
WHO
WHAT
WHERE
WHY
WHEN
HOW
WHO
WHAT
WHERE
WHY
WHEN
HOW

This page from the abolitionist paper *The Liberator* was published by William Lloyd Garrison in 1831.

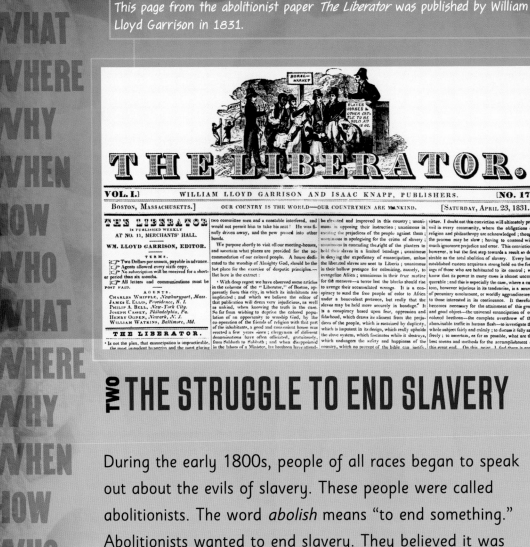

TWO THE STRUGGLE TO END SLAVERY

During the early 1800s, people of all races began to speak out about the evils of slavery. These people were called abolitionists. The word *abolish* means "to end something." Abolitionists wanted to end slavery. They believed it was wrong to own other people. For many years, abolitionists had a hard time getting many white Americans to join their cause.

Some supporters of slavery argued that ending it would be too hard. How would plantation owners find enough workers for their fields? Where would all the freed slaves go? How would they find jobs and homes?

Some people said that freed slaves would kill their former owners. These people believed that slavery was needed to keep white people safe.

Defenders of slavery also claimed that the U.S. government could not tell the states what to do about slavery. They thought each state should decide for itself.

Abolitionists disagreed with these arguments. They worked to change the way people thought about slavery. Many abolitionists published newspapers and pamphlets. They gave speeches and asked people to sign letters to Congress that called for a ban of slavery. Some abolitionists also helped slaves escape to freedom. Some refused to buy goods or food that had been produced by slave labor.

Bostonians listen to abolitionist Wendell Phillips speaking out against slavery in the 1800s.

ABOLITIONIST ELIJAH LOVEJOY

In many places, supporters of slavery often beat abolitionists. The attackers wanted to stop abolitionists from sharing their ideas. Some abolitionists were murdered. A newspaper editor named Elijah Lovejoy was one of them. Lovejoy printed newspapers about his abolitionist views in Missouri and Illinois. Three times, an angry mob broke into his building (right) and destroyed his printing press. Without a press, Lovejoy couldn't print his newspaper. Each time, he found a way to get a new press. The fourth attack took place in 1837 in Alton, Illinois. This time the mob shot and killed Lovejoy.

Most northern whites didn't want slavery to expand, or spread, into new areas. But more Americans were moving westward and building settlements. So the disagreements about slavery went westward too.

Congress argued many times over whether new states and |territories| should allow slavery. These arguments weren't just about whether slavery was right or wrong. They were about power.

> large areas of land that do not have the full rights of a state

When a new state entered the United States, it gained the power to send representatives and senators to Congress. At the end of 1819, the number of free states equaled the number of slave states. But new states and territories were being added all the time. Each side worried that the other side would gain more members of Congress than its side had. Then Congress might pass laws that only one side wanted.

In 1820 this worry was settled for a while by the Missouri Compromise. Congress allowed Missouri to enter the United States as a slave state. At the same time, Maine entered as a free state. The compromise also stated that slavery would not be permitted in any area north of Missouri's southern boundary, other than Missouri itself.

Meanwhile, the abolitionist movement was getting stronger. One of the most important U.S. abolitionists knew a lot about slavery. That's because he had been a slave himself. Frederick Douglass grew up as a slave in Baltimore, Maryland. There, his owner's wife taught him the alphabet. Douglass then got white children in the neighborhood to teach him to read.

He read newspapers and books. Douglass learned that in the North, he could be free. In 1838 Douglass escaped to Massachusetts. He was twenty years old. He gave speeches about his life as a slave. His deep voice, strong feelings, and amazing way with words made him a great speaker.

"No man can put a chain about the ankle of his fellow man without...finding the other end fastened about his own neck."
—speech at an abolitionist meeting, 1883

Frederick Douglass

Douglass wrote a book to tell his story. It was published in 1845. The book described the horrors of slavery. It was so well written that it changed the minds of many white people who thought that black people weren't intelligent.

Douglass and other abolitionists worked hard for their cause. Many white people in the North disliked slavery. But they didn't think slavery should be ended in states where it already existed. They felt that slaves were truly the property of their owners.

Congress faced another problem in 1848. That year the United States defeated Mexico in the Mexican-American War (1846–1848). The slave state of Texas gained land as a result. Northerners didn't want slavery to expand into the new parts of Texas. Congress passed the Compromise of 1850 to solve this problem. It created the territories of New Mexico and Utah from parts of the new land. These territories

OREGON TERRITORY

CALIFORNIA

UTAH TERRITORY

THE COMPROMISE OF 1850

NEW MEXICO TERRITORY

TEXAS

Two runaway slaves were captured in Boston and returned to South Carolina under the new Fugitive Slave Act. This illustration originally appeared in a book published in 1898.

were not part of Texas. Their citizens would make their own decisions about slavery. At the same time, California would be admitted as a free state.

Why would the slave states give up so much? In exchange, they got a new law that protected slave owners throughout the United States. The Fugitive Slave Act of 1850 required U.S. officials to capture anyone who might be a slave on the run. A person arrested under this law would be sent to the slave owner in the South. A hearing would be held. The hearing would decide what should happen to the captured person. But that person could not speak at the hearing.

The Fugitive Slave Act didn't apply only in slave states. It applied in free states too. This law made it harder for slaves to reach freedom by going to the North.

a meeting at which an accused person can appear and be heard

NEBRASKA
TERRITORY

KANSAS
TERRITORY

SLAVERY
PROHIBITED

DECISION
LEFT TO
TERRITORIES

SLAVERY
PERMITTED

KANSAS-NEBRASKA
ACT, 1854

It also meant that slaves who made it to freedom in the North could be caught and sent back into slavery. Even black people who had never been slaves could be arrested and sent South!

The defenders of slavery had another victory in 1854. Congress passed the Kansas-Nebraska Act. It created two new territories, Kansas and Nebraska. In those places, citizens would decide about slavery by voting. And any new territories that entered the United States would do the same thing.

But what about the Missouri Compromise? It had said that slavery would not expand north of Missouri's southern border. The Kansas-Nebraska Act undid that part of the law. Slavery could expand to new areas that were not part of the South if people voted to allow it.

Settlers poured into Kansas. People from both sides of the argument rushed to become part of the voting process. Violence sprang up between the two groups. The territory became known as Bleeding Kansas.

The anger grew after a U.S. Supreme Court decision in 1857. Dred Scott was a slave. He went to court to sue for his freedom. His owner had taken him into the free state of Illinois and the free territory of Minnesota. Scott argued that when he entered those areas, he was protected by their laws. He thought his slavery had ended when his owner took him to the North.

The court did not agree. The judges declared that no African who had been brought into the United States as a slave could ever be a citizen. Neither could such a person's children or grandchildren. Even free African Americans could not be citizens. Since black people weren't citizens, they weren't protected by the laws of any state. They also could not sue in court.

The Supreme Court didn't stop there. It ruled that Congress shouldn't have tried to use the Missouri Compromise to outlaw slavery in the northern territories. The court said that went against the Constitution.

Dred Scott

In fact, not even the citizens of those territories could vote to ban slavery.

The Dred Scott decision outraged people throughout the North. If all new territories had to allow slavery, what would happen when those territories became states? There would be many more slave states than free states. Those new slave states would send representatives to Congress. Then Congress would have far more members who wanted to expand slavery. Would Congress try to make slavery legal even in the North? Would the Supreme Court try to do so?

Meanwhile, a few abolitionists grew impatient. They had tried to end slavery peacefully. But they had gotten nowhere. Some of these people turned to violence. In Bleeding Kansas, John Brown and his sons murdered five proslavery men in 1856. Then, in 1859, Brown led a raid on an arms storehouse at Harpers Ferry, Virginia. His goal was to steal weapons from the town. Brown planned to arm the

John Brown

"Now, if it is deemed necessary that I should forfeit my life for the furtherance... of justice, ... I submit: so let it be done!"
—last speech to the court, 1859

John Brown leaves the courthouse at Harpers Ferry after being found guilty of treason and murder. This is a copy of an original painting by Thomas Hovenden (1840–1895).

area's slaves and start a rebellion. The plan failed. Brown was put on trial for treason and murder. He was found guilty and hanged.

Slave owners throughout the South were terrified. Would there be more violence? At the same time, the presidential election of 1860 was approaching. Who could possibly lead the nation through this dark time?

NEXT QUESTION

WHAT EVENTS HAD SHAPED THE NEW PRESIDENT'S FEELINGS ABOUT SLAVERY?

Abraham Lincoln, wearing blue pants on the left, saw the sale of a slave woman in New Orleans in 1831. This scene was depicted by Joseph Boggs Beale (1841–1926).

THREE A NEW PRESIDENT AND A NEW HOPE

The man who would lead the nation through its turning point had strong feelings about slavery. Abraham Lincoln was born in 1809 in the slave state of Kentucky. As a boy, he moved with his family to Indiana, a free state. Years later, he made a trip to New Orleans, a city in the slave state of Louisiana. There he saw an African American woman being sold at a market. Men called out prices. The woman was sold for the highest price.

That sight stayed with Lincoln for the rest of his life. He decided that "if slavery is not wrong, nothing is wrong." But he wasn't an abolitionist. He didn't think that a quick end to slavery could work. Slave owners had too much at stake. They would never let the government take away the people they thought of as their property.

Besides, Lincoln didn't believe that the U.S. government had the right to end slavery. He thought that each state should solve the problem on its own. Lincoln hoped that as years passed, slavery would end one state at a time.

Lincoln was different from the abolitionists in another way. Many abolitionists believed that black people were the equals of white people. For instance, they thought both groups were equally intelligent. They also believed both groups could tell right from wrong. These abolitionists felt that blacks should have the same rights as whites. For example, black men should have the right to vote, just as white men did.

"If slavery is not wrong, nothing is wrong."

Abraham Lincoln

A HOUSE DIVIDED AGAINST ITSELF

During the late 1850s, Lincoln came to believe that slavery wasn't just wrong. It also posed a threat to the country. He explained his thinking in a speech in June 1858: "'A house divided against itself cannot stand.' I believe this government cannot endure, permanently half slave and half free. I do not expect the Union to be dissolved—I do not expect the house to fall—but I do expect it will cease to be divided. It will become all one thing, or all the other." No one knew then how right Lincoln was when he spoke these words.

(Women could not vote at this time.) And black people should be able to get the same jobs and education as white people.

Lincoln didn't agree. He said in 1858 that he believed white people were better than blacks. And he thought the two groups would never be able to live together as equals. At the same time, he believed that African Americans should have "the right to life, liberty, and the pursuit of happiness."

Lincoln was no abolitionist. Still, he strongly opposed [was against] the growth of slavery in new parts of the country. He had also become known for his careful way of thinking. He could talk about slavery in ways that many people understood. In 1860 Lincoln defeated three other men to become president of the United States.

Lincoln didn't win in a single southern state. Many white people in the South believed that, as president, Lincoln would end slavery. Even before he took office, seven southern states decided to leave the United States. They wanted to form their own country.

An 1860 campaign button for Abraham Lincoln and his running mate, Hannibal Hamlin

Four other southern states joined them later. They called their country the Confederate States of America. Lincoln faced a terrible problem from the first moment he was president.

NEXT QUESTION

HOW COULD LINCOLN SAVE THE UNITED STATES OF AMERICA?

President-elect Lincoln takes the oath of office at his inauguration in March 1861.

FOUR DIVIDED BY WAR

a promise a person makes to speak the truth or to keep a promise

When Abraham Lincoln became president in March 1861, he swore an oath to support and defend the Constitution. That oath decided his reaction to the secession of the southern states. The

leaving a political union

Constitution didn't allow states to leave the United States. As a result, Lincoln refused to recognize the Confederacy as a separate country. He described the southern states as rebels who should return to the Union.

The Constitution didn't give Lincoln much help on the question of slavery, though. Remember, it didn't directly mention slavery at all. Lincoln felt sure that the

Constitution didn't allow the president to make laws about slavery. He still thought that each state ought to make its own decision. Although he hated slavery, he couldn't end it on his own.

Meanwhile, he had a war to fight. On April 12, 1861, Confederate troops opened fire on Fort Sumter, a U.S. army fort in South Carolina. The Civil War (1861–1865) had begun.

The first months of the war didn't go well for the Union. It lost several important battles. And the Union army failed to march into Confederate territory.

WHERE IS FORT SUMTER?
It is in the harbor of Charleston, South Carolina.

This print, published by Currier & Ives in 1861, depicts the bombing of Fort Sumter at the start of the Civil War.

Before the war, slaves in New Orleans get bales of cotton ready to load onto ships bound for Europe. During the war, the Union blocked such shipments.

Soon Lincoln had a new worry. The Confederacy wanted the support of other countries, such as Great Britain and France. Those countries needed shipments of cotton from the South to make cloth. But the Union had blocked the South's ports with warships. What if the British or the French gave money, weapons, or even troops to the South? Then the Union would have an even harder time. It might lose the war.

How could Lincoln keep Great Britain and France out of the war? One idea had to do with slavery. The British and French had once taken part in the slave trade. But slavery became illegal in almost all Great Britain in 1833. France banned slavery in 1848. Lincoln wondered if he should make the war a quest to free slaves as well as to save the Union. Then the British and French might not help the Confederacy.

What about the Constitution? It didn't give the president the power to end slavery. But it did make the president the commander in chief of the U.S. military. And it gave him more power during times of war. Lincoln knew that the South needed the labor of slaves to win the war. He realized that he could free slaves as a way of striking against the rebels.

Then again, freeing the slaves might create a new problem for the Union. Several slave states had not joined the Confederacy. Delaware, Kentucky, Missouri, and Maryland had stayed with the Union. These states were called border states. Most of them shared a border with both the Confederacy and the Union. They provided troops for the Union. And the army used them as bases for attacks on the South. The northwestern part of Virginia had stayed with the Union too.

MARYLAND

DELAWARE

MISSOURI

WEST VIRGINIA

KENTUCKY

BORDER STATES

If Lincoln freed the slaves, the border states might leave the Union to keep their slaves. Their troops, weapons, and land would become part of the Confederacy. Then the Union would almost certainly lose the war. Lincoln had to make sure that wouldn't happen.

PRESIDENT LINCOLN'S LETTER

Abraham Lincoln made clear his thoughts about ending slavery in a letter he sent in August 1862, only a few months before the Emancipation Proclamation. He wrote, "If I could save the Union without freeing any slave I would do it, and if I could save it by freeing all the slaves I would do it; and if I could save it by freeing some and leaving others alone I would also do that. What I do about slavery, and the colored [African American] race, I do because I believe it helps to save the Union...." Lincoln meant that keeping the United States a single nation was his one and only goal during the Civil War. It wasn't his goal to end slavery, even though he hated it. He wanted more than anything else to save the country.

During the summer of 1862, Lincoln made up his mind. He would free the slaves in the South but not in the border states. He worried that the border states might leave the Union anyway. They might feel sorry for slave owners in the South. Lincoln decided not to announce his order right away. He would wait until the Union had won an important battle. Then the border states would be sure that the Union would win the war. They wouldn't risk joining the Confederacy.

In September 1862, the Battle of Antietam gave Lincoln the chance he needed. This bloody battle took place in Maryland.

A print produced in 1888 by Kurz & Allison Publishers shows soldiers from the North and South fighting each other during the Battle of Antietam.

More than six thousand soldiers died at Antietam. Still, it was a win for the North.

Lincoln made the most of it. On September 22, he announced the first part of the Emancipation Proclamation. On January 1, 1863, slaves in any state that was fighting against the Union would be freed. Southern states had one hundred days to return to the United States. If they didn't, owners would lose their slaves.

Not a single state in the Confederacy returned. The war went on. On New Year's Day 1863, Abraham Lincoln signed the second and final part of the Emancipation Proclamation.

NEXT QUESTION

WHERE WERE THE FIRST SLAVES WHO WERE FREED BY THE EMANCIPATION PROCLAMATION?

WHO
WHAT
WHERE
WHY
WHEN
HOW
WHO
WHAT
WHERE
WHY
WHEN
HOW
WHO
WHAT
WHERE
WHY
WHEN
HOW

Lincoln reads his draft of the Emancipation Proclamation to his presidential advisers in this painting by U.S. artist Alonzo Chappel (1828–1887).

FIVE FREEDOM FOR SOME

As President Lincoln had planned, his order didn't free all the slaves in the country. It freed only those who lived in states that had left the Union. Slaves who lived in states that had stayed in the Union remained slaves.

Lincoln left out other slaves too. Union troops had already taken over several parts of the Confederacy when he issued the order. The slaves in most of those places were not freed.

How could the North make the South obey the Emancipation Proclamation? Could the slaves in the Confederate states be set free by a piece of paper?

Their owners didn't accept Lincoln's words as law. They followed their own government.

That's why slave owners couldn't be forced to give up their slaves until Union troops took over their homes. So the Emancipation Proclamation actually freed very few slaves at first. Only about twenty thousand out of the four million slaves held throughout the United States were freed.

Even so, January 1, 1863, was a day of joy for all who had worked to end slavery. It was especially joyful for former slaves. Henry M. Turner, an African American minister, lived in Washington, D.C., when Lincoln's order was announced. He grabbed a newspaper and rushed to his church. "I ran as if for my life," he remembered later. "When the people saw me coming with the paper in my hand they raised a shouting cheer."

Throughout the Union, telegraph wires carried the news to one city after another. Both African Americans and white people celebrated with singing, dancing, prayers, and feasts. Bells rang out and cannons were fired to honor Lincoln's decision. In Boston three thousand people gathered at Tremont Temple.

telegraph a system for sending messages electronically through wires or radio

"I ran as if for my life. When the people saw me coming with the paper in my hand they raised a shouting cheer."

Henry M. Turner

THE SEA ISLANDS SLAVES

The Emancipation Proclamation freed twenty thousand slaves right away. About half lived on the Sea Islands off the coast of South Carolina. This area's white residents had left in late 1861. That's when Union troops arrived by sea. The ten thousand slaves who stayed formed a new community. They took over the plantations. Several hundred abolitionists arrived from the North. They supported the slaves with schools and a hospital. The worst horrors of the past had ended for the Sea Islands slaves. But they were not officially free until Lincoln's proclamation.

Frederick Douglass spoke. He thanked God that he had lived to see slavery end. The cheering, music, and speeches went on until almost dawn the next morning.

The Emancipation Proclamation changed the war as Lincoln had hoped it would. Great Britain and France did not help the Confederacy. Some Union troops were against freeing the slaves. But for many soldiers, their new cause made

An engraving by J. W. Watts in 1864 shows a soldier reading the Emancipation Proclamation to a group of slaves.

Twenty-seven African American soldiers of Company E pose with rifles at Fort Lincoln in Washington, D.C.

the war more meaningful. As they moved farther into the South, the U.S. Army freed slaves everywhere they found them. Many former slaves became soldiers and joined the fight to free others.

As the Union won more and more battles, people wondered whether the Emancipation Proclamation would stay in effect forever. It had been a wartime order, after all. When the war ended, would Lincoln's orders end too? Would the South be allowed to have slaves again?

NEXT QUESTION

WHAT ABOUT THE SLAVES IN THE BORDER STATES? WHEN WOULD THEY BE FREED?

WHO
WHAT
WHERE
WHY
WHEN
HOW
WHO
WHAT
WHERE
WHY
WHEN
HOW
WHO
WHAT
WHERE
WHY
WHEN
HOW

Freed after the announcement of the Emancipation Proclamation, hundreds of slaves left their former homesteads and hoped to build a new life somewhere else.

SIX FREEDOM FOR ALL

Lincoln had thought about these questions too. He worked with Congress to make a change to the Constitution. This type of change is called an amendment. The Thirteenth Amendment ended slavery forever throughout the United States. It was passed by Congress on February 1, 1865. But it could not become law until three-fourths of the states approved it.

Some of the border states had already ended slavery by this time. Maryland, Missouri, and Tennessee freed their slaves by early 1865. West Virginia had become a state in 1863. It ended slavery in early February 1865, just two days after Congress passed the Thirteenth Amendment.

A few months later, the Civil War ended too. The Confederacy surrendered in June 1865. President Lincoln did not live to see this final victory. He was killed on April 14, 1865, by John Wilkes Booth.

Some people remained slaves in areas controlled by the South until the very end of the war.

THE THIRTEENTH AMENDMENT

Congress approved the Thirteenth Amendment in 1865. It had been more than sixty years since an amendment to the Constitution had been approved. The Thirteenth Amendment forbids slavery and "involuntary servitude." That means forcing people to work against their will. The amendment includes one exception. People who are convicted of crimes can be forced to work as part of their punishment. The Supreme Court also ruled in 1918 that the Thirteenth Amendment does not apply to the military draft. In a draft, the government requires people to serve in the military. A draft usually happens only when the military needs more soldiers in an emergency, such as a war.

John Wilkes Booth shot President Lincoln while he was attending a play at Ford's Theater in Washington, D.C., on April 14, 1865.

A famous story about these slaves inspired a new holiday. Union troops arrived in Galveston, Texas, on June 18, 1865. On June 19, General Gordon Granger read Lincoln's order to a group of slaves. A year later, the former slaves gathered to honor the anniversary of their freedom. This was the first of many Juneteenth celebrations. The holiday is still marked across the United States.

More time was needed for slaves to gain freedom in two states. Slavery remained legal in Kentucky and Delaware until December 1865. That's when enough states approved the Thirteenth Amendment to make it the law of the land.

With the end of slavery and the war, Americans tried to make a new beginning. Union troops had destroyed many homes, farms, and towns in the South. For the former slaves, life wasn't easy. Some moved to the North or the Southwest

On June 19, 1865, General Gordon Granger (right) read the news about Lincoln ending slavery to a group of newly freed slaves in Texas.

This photgraph of a family of sharecroppers was taken around 1890. Sharecropping was a way for newly freed slaves to farm without having to buy land.

to look for jobs and a new home. Some stayed in the South. They worked and searched for loved ones who had been sold away. Former slaves were paid for their labor. But the pay was low. Few could buy land to start their own farms. Instead, they worked fields owned by white men—sometimes their former masters.

Many of these workers became sharecroppers. A sharecropper worked the owner's fields in exchange for part of the crop. In most cases, sharecroppers' portions were small. They couldn't earn much money. But they felt they had no choice. To survive, they had to take whatever work they were offered for whatever pay they were offered.

Still, African Americans made the most of their new chances. Throughout the country, they started schools for their children. They also set up their own churches and newspapers. Some started their own towns. Places such as Mound Bayou, Mississippi, and Langston in the Oklahoma Territory grew into communities where black people could live in peace. They ran their own businesses. And they avoided many of the dangers and insults of racism.

The struggle for equal rights for people of all races certainly didn't end with the Emancipation Proclamation. In fact, that struggle continues to this day. But for African Americans, the first step on this long journey began with the end of slavery.

This school for African American students was in Carlisle, Pennsylvania.

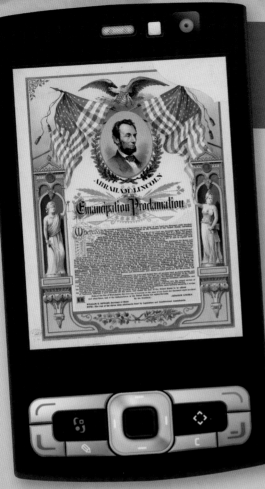

This print of the Emancipation Proclamation, created in 1888, pictures two U.S. flags and an eagle over a portrait of President Lincoln.

The man who made the greatest single contribution to that first step was not an abolitionist. He didn't free all the slaves. He didn't even believe that the races were equal. But he did hate slavery with all his heart. And he found a way to do what he could to stop it while reuniting the nation. For these reasons, many Americans remember Abraham Lincoln as a hero and one of the greatest presidents in our history.

NEXT QUESTION

HOW DO WE KNOW SO MUCH ABOUT THE EMANCIPATION PROCLAMATION?

Primary Source: The Emancipation Proclamation

The best way to see into the past and learn about any historical event is with primary sources. Primary sources are created near the time being studied. Some primary sources are firsthand accounts of events in history. Others provide information in different ways. Letters, journals, newspaper articles, and political documents are examples of primary sources. Many people who lived during the time of slavery in North America left behind writings that help us understand the past. The captains of ships that brought kidnapped Africans to North America often kept journals about their trips. Some former slaves, such as Frederick Douglass and Harriet Jacobs, wrote books that described their experiences. Slave owners kept records of the names and numbers of people they bought and sold. Abolitionists published newspaper articles and pamphlets that told of the cruelties of slavery. All these writings are important primary sources.

The primary source below is a section from the Emancipation Proclamation. In it, Abraham Lincoln declares certain slaves free. He also makes suggestions about what they should do with their freedom.

I do order and declare that all persons held as slaves within said designated States, and parts of States, are, and henceforward shall be free; and that the Executive government of the United States . . . will recognize and maintain the freedom of said persons.

And I hereby enjoin upon [urge] the people so declared to be free to abstain from [avoid] all violence, unless in necessary self-defence; and I recommend to them that, in all cases when allowed, they labor faithfully for reasonable wages.

And I further declare and make known, that such persons of suitable condition, will be received into the armed service of the United States. . . .

TELL YOUR ABOLITIONIST STORY

Imagine that you are an abolitionist in 1860. Write a speech that you will give to a group of people who support slavery.

WHO are you? (Are you a boy, a girl, a man, or a woman?)

WHY do you believe slavery is wrong?

WHEN did you make this decision?

WHERE should slaves live after they are freed?

WHAT jobs will they get?

HOW should people who owned slaves run their farms and plantations without them?

Some of the information you will need is in this book. But you might need to do research in the library or on the Internet.

USE **WHO, WHAT, WHERE, WHY, WHEN,** AND **HOW** TO THINK OF OTHER QUESTIONS TO HELP YOU WRITE YOUR SPEECH!

Timeline

1500s
European traders begin kidnapping Africans and selling them into slavery in Europe and elsewhere.

1619
Africans arrive in America for the first time. In Jamestown, Virginia, a trader sells about twenty Africans into slavery.

1641
Massachusetts becomes the first American colony to officially make slavery legal.

1662
Virginia passes a law declaring that children born to women slaves are slaves themselves.

1776
The **Declaration of Independence** declares that "all men are created equal." Yet every British colony in North America permits slavery.

1777
Vermont becomes the first colony to ban slavery. Other northern colonies follow.

1788
The U.S. Constitution is ratified (approved). Slavery remains legal.

1793
An invention called the cotton gin makes farming cotton very profitable in parts of the South. The need for labor increases, and the number of slaves increases as well.

1808
Congress bans the international slave trade, meaning that slaves can no longer be brought from Africa. Some traders continue to smuggle Africans into the United States.

1820

The Missouri Compromise admits Maine to the United States as a free state and Missouri as a slave state. Slavery is banned in territories north of Missouri's southern border.

1850

The Compromise of 1850 creates the territories of Arizona and New Mexico, admits California as a free state, and makes the **Fugitive Slave Act** a law.

1854

The Kansas-Nebraska Act reverses the Missouri Compromise, leading to violence in Kansas.

1857

The U.S. Supreme Court rules in the Dred Scott case that slaves and former slaves are not citizens and that slavery cannot be restricted in U.S. territories.

300 DOLLARS

REWARD!

RUNAWAY from John S. Doak on the 21st inst., two NEGRO MEN; LOGAN 45 years of age, bald-headed, one or more crooked fingers; DAN 21 years old, six feet high. Both black. I will pay ONE HUNDRED DOLLARS for the apprehension and delivery of LOGAN, or to have him confined so that I can get him. I will also pay TWO HUNDRED DOLLARS for the apprehension of DAN, or to have him confined so that I can get him.
JOHN S. DOAKE,
Springfield, Mo., April 24th, 1857.

1860

Abraham Lincoln is elected president. In December, South Carolina becomes the first state to secede.

1861

Seven southern states form the Confederate States of America in February, later joined by four others. Lincoln takes office in March. The Civil War begins in April.

1862

A Union victory in the Battle of Antietam gives Lincoln an opening to issue the first part of the Emancipation Proclamation in September.

1863

On January 1, Lincoln issues the second part of the Emancipation Proclamation. About twenty thousand slaves are immediately freed.

1864

Lincoln is elected to a second term.

1865

Lincoln is assassinated in April. The Civil War officially ends in June. Slavery ends for good throughout the United States with the approval of the Thirteenth Amendment in December.

Source Notes

8   Dorothy Schneider and Carl J. Schneider, *Slavery in America* (New York: Facts on File, 2007), 129.

16 Beck, Emily Morison, ed. *Bartlett's Familiar Quotations*. 15th ed. Boston: Little, Brown and Company: 1980.

20 Ibid.

22 Michael P. Johnson, ed., *Abraham Lincoln, Slavery, and the Civil War: Selected Writings and Speeches* (Boston: Bedford/St. Martin's, 2001), 285.

23 Ibid.

24 Ibid., 63.

24 Ibid., 72.

30 Ibid., 205.

33 James Oliver Horton and Lois E. Horton, *Slavery and the Making of America* (New York: Oxford University Press, 2005), 187.

33 Ibid.

37 National Archives and Records Administration, "Transcript of the 13th Amendment to the U.S. Constitution: Abolition of Slavery (1865)," Our Documents, n.d., http://www.ourdocuments.gov/doc.php?flash=false&doc=40&page=transcript (July 12, 2009).

42 National Archives and Records Administration, "The Emancipation Proclamation," n.d. http://www.archives.gov/exhibits/featured_documents/emancipation_proclamation/transcript.html (July 12, 2009).

Selected Bibliography

Davis, David Brion. *Inhuman Bondage: The Rise and Fall of Slavery in the New World*. New York: Oxford University Press, 2006.

Franklin, John Hope. *The Emancipation Proclamation*. Garden City, NY: Doubleday & Company, 1963.

Holzer, Harold, Edna Greene Medford, and Frank J. Williams. *The Emancipation Proclamation: Three Views*. Baton Rouge: Louisiana State University Press, 2006.

Horton, James Oliver, and Lois E. Horton. *Slavery and the Making of America*. New York: Oxford University Press, 2005.

Johnson, Michael P., ed. *Abraham Lincoln, Slavery, and the Civil War: Selected Writings and Speeches*. Boston: Bedford/St. Martin's, 2001.

Klingaman, William K. *Abraham Lincoln and the Road to Emancipation, 1861–1865*. New York: Viking Penguin, 2001.

Schneider, Dorothy, and Carl J. Schneider. *Slavery in America*. New York: Facts on File, 2007.

Trefousse, Hans L. *Lincoln's Decision for Emancipation*. Philadelphia: J. B. Lippincott Company, 1975.

Further Reading

Landau, Elaine. *The Emancipation Proclamation: Would You Do What Lincoln Did?* Berkeley Heights, NJ: Enslow Elementary, 2008. This book asks readers to take on the roles of different figures in the Civil War and determine what they would have done in their situations.

McComb, Marianne. *The Emancipation Proclamation*. Washington, DC: National Geographic Society, 2006. This book describes what the proclamation did and did not do and presents the full text of the Emancipation Proclamation as well as the Thirteenth Amendment.

Nelson, Vaunda Micheaux, and Drew Nelson. *Juneteenth*. Minneapolis: Millbrook Press, 2005. This illustrated book tells the true story of the first Juneteenth and how the holiday is celebrated in modern times.

Schott, Jane A. *Abraham Lincoln*. Minneapolis: Lerner Publications Company, 2003. From his boyhood to his assassination, this biography brings to life the story of one of the greatest American presidents.

Welch, Catherine A. *Frederick Douglass*. Minneapolis: Lerner Publications Company, 2003. The great abolitionist's escape from slavery and rise to fame as a speaker and writer form the basis of this biography.

Websites

Born in Slavery: Slave Narratives from the Federal Writers' Project, 1936–38
http://lcweb2.loc.gov/ammem/snhtml/snhome.html
This site contains more than 2,300 accounts of slavery, given during the 1930s by people who had lived as slaves. Viewers can search the accounts by keyword or browse by the names of states or the names of the former slaves.

Discovery School: Understanding Slavery
http://school.discoveryeducation.com/schooladventures/slavery/
Visitors to this site can learn about the history of slavery throughout the world and experience a slave auction.

Frederick Douglass National Historic Site Virtual Exhibit
http://www.nps.gov/history/museum/exhibits/douglass/
The life, accomplishments, and final home of Frederick Douglass are showcased in this National Park Service website.

Lincoln Papers: Emancipation Proclamation
http://lcweb2.loc.gov/ammem/alhtml/almintr.html
The Library of Congress and the Lincoln Studies Center at Knox College have placed many important examples of Lincoln's papers on this site, including the Emancipation Proclamation.

Index

Photo Acknowledgments

The images in this book are used with the permission of: © iStockphoto.com/DNY59, p. 1; © Erik De Graaf/Dreamstime.com, p. 1 (background) and all rusty chain backgrounds; © iStockphoto.com/sx70, pp. 3 (top), 8 (bottom), 14 (left), 24, 30, 34 (top), 37 (top); © iStockphoto.com/Ayse Nazli Deliormanli, pp. 3 (bottom), 43 (left); © iStockphoto.com/Serdar Yagci, pp. 4–5 (background), 43 (background); © Bill Hauser/Independent Picture Service, pp. 4–5 (top), 16, 18, 27 (inset), 29; © SuperStock/SuperStock, pp. 4–5 (bottom), 5 (inset), 8 (top), 9, 21 (top), 44, 45; © iStockphoto.com/Andrey Pustovoy, pp. 5 (bottom right), 25 (top), 41 (top); Library of Congress, pp. 6 (LC-DIG-ppmsca-05933), 15 (LC-USZ62-15887), 19 (LC-USZ62-5092), 23 (LC-USZC4-2439), 25 (inset) (LC-DIG-ppmsca-19430), 26 (LC-USZ62-22734), 27 (bottom) (LC-DIG-ppmsca-19520), 31 (top) (LC-DIG-pga-01841), 35 (top) (LC-DIG-cwpb-04294), 36 (LC-USZ62-112158), 37 (bottom) (LC-USZ62-4608), 41 (inset) (LC-DIG-pga-02797), 43 (right) (LC-DIG-pga-01556); © Hulton Archive/Getty Images, p. 7; © North Wind Picture Archives, pp. 10, 13, 14 (right), 17, 28, 33; © Bettmann/CORBIS, p. 12; The Art Archive/Culver Pictures, p. 20; © George Eastman House/Hulton Archive/Getty Images, pp. 22, 34 (bottom); © iStockphoto.com/Talshiar, p. 27 (top); The Art Archive/Museum of Fine Arts Boston/Granger Collection, p. 32; The Granger Collection, New York, pp. 38, 39; The Art Archive, p. 40.

Front cover: © George Eastman House/Hulton Archive/Getty Images.